POETRY BY ANTONIA WANG:

IN ENGLISH:

Love Bites: Poetry & Prose (2019)

In the Posh Cocoon: Poetry and Bits of Life (2020)

Hindsight 2020: Brief Reflections on a Long Year (2021)

Palette: Love Poems and Painted Words (2022)

Things I Could Have Said in One Line But Didn't:
Poems on Love, Relationships and Existentialism (2023)

Taste of Salt: Poems on Love and Life (2024)

Healing (From Everything, All the Time):
Poetry and Vignettes (2025)

IN SPANISH:

Retrospectiva 2020: Reflexiones breves sobre un año largo (2021)

Matices: Poemas de amor y paisajes del alma (2023)

Rincones barridos: Poesías del interior (2023)

Healing (From Everything, All the Time): Poetry and Vignettes
Copyright © 2025, Antonia Wang

All rights reserved. No part of this book may be stored in a retrieval system, transmitted in any form or reproduced by any means, electronic, mechanical, photocopying, recording, or otherwise without the written consent of the author, except in the case of brief quotations included in critical articles and reviews.

Any names, locations, organizations, and products have been used in a fictitious context. Any resemblance to actual persons, or places is purely coincidental.

Without in any way limiting the author's exclusive rights under copyright, any use of this publication to train generative artificial intelligence (AI) technologies to generate text is expressly prohibited. The author reserves all rights to license uses of this work for generative AI training and development of machine learning language models.

FIRST EDITION

Paperback ISBN: 979-8-9903875-1-5
Ebook ISBN: 979-8-9903875-2-2

Written by Antonia Wang
Edited by Vanessa Anderson

www.biteslove.com

Healing

(FROM EVERYTHING, ALL THE TIME)

Poetry and Vignettes
ANTONIA WANG

"The wound is the place
where the light enters you."

— Rumi

Contents

Prologue	17
Evergreen Fandango	19
Rewind	20
Forging Light	21
Forward	22
Eden	23
Desert Stones	24
A Silent Banquet	25
I Shush My Loud Heart	27
Sacrificial Lamb	28
Undercurrent	29
Play Dough	30
Tidal Draw	31
The Pail of Whispers	32
Pixelated Embrace	33
Subtle Victory	34
For Lily	35
Gangrene	36
To the IKEA Mannequin on My Shelf	37
Shifting Eyes	38
Out There, the World	39
Liquid Suspension	40
Doom's Overture	41
I Always Come Up Empty	42
Sepia Stains	43
I Let Love Happen	44

Cataclysm	45
Where Did the Clouds Go?	46
Hispaniola	47
Petals and Stars	48
Harmonies	49
Flowing with the Stream	50
Sometimes We Die	51
Release Me	52
Shallow Grave	53
Within	54
Inertia	55
Dharma	56
Portrait of a Missing Kiss	57
Time to Uncover	58
Hollow Ritual	59
Brisk Awakening	60
Neptune's Womb	61
Winter's Touch	62
Lilith's Mark	63
Golden Beach Sojourn	65
Once a Mermaid	66
Thanksgiving	67
Through Broken Gates	68
Belated Thanks	69
Pine Cones and Tree Lights	70
Christmas in Quisqueya	71
Two Dolls and Three Kings	73
The Art of Unbinding	77
Mindfulness	79
Mouths Open, Slowly Sipping	80

Holly	81
Little Mercies	82
Pinecone Vernacular	83
The Forgotten Snow	84
Soul Soaking	85
Elegy of a Passing Wish	86
Borrowed Time	87
When You Return	89
Urgency of the Unhealed	90
Untapped Shores	91
Head Stand	92
Power Play	93
From Derrière to Amber Coast	94
More than Skin	95
Conjuring Beauty	96
Sweet Mortality	97
Undeniable	98
Screens and Shadows	99
Past the Naked Tree	100
Molting the Rough	101
Promised Land	102
Yogi Freedom Ride	103
Liminal Gaze	104
Evil Eye	105
Drowning Weight	106
Bewilderment of Moon	107
White-winged Serenade	108
What Does it Take to Keep a Soul Alive?	109
Entanglements	110
It Daws and Redawns	111

Year of the Dragon	112
Living for the Chase	113
Riding the Milky Way	114
Broken Record	115
Whispers of the Watershed	116
Drafting the Improbable	117
Sulking with the Missing Bloom	118
Limping Devils	119
Offering	120
Emissaries of the Unsaid	121
An Ocean of Sky	122
Tame Under the Live Oak	123
Almost Love	124
Intimacy if a Doting Genie	125
Unknotted	126
La Colombe	127
Battle's Yield	128
Quiet Quitting of the Housewife	129
Moon Hisses Behind the Clouds	130
Crushed Under my Soles	131
Rolling the Hours	132
A Pinch of Oregano	133
Return of the Sea Goddess	134
Acts of Service as My Love Language	135
Unbowed	136
Ice Fossil	137
The Matrix Reloads	138
Compost	139
Fatigued by the Ephemeral	140
Fair-weather Hymn	141

Blocked Throat Chakra	142
Wayward Vessels	143
Spring Cleaning	144
The Catalyst	145
Fundamental Flaw	146
Bribing Destiny	147
After the Rain	148
Wild and Fruitless	149
Proof of Love	150
Empty Tomb	151
Beyond the Treshold	152
Curves of the Lemniscate	153
Grasshopers Exhale	154
Severed Radicle	155
Lament of Endless Starts	156
The Hand We Were Dealt	157
A Besotted Star	158
Seeds of Revelation	159
Clockwork of Memory	160
The View from the Islet	161
Serendipity	162
Dead-air Magenta	163
Summer Slopes	164
Aftershock of Reverence	165
Making a Mark	166
Immortals' Play	167
If It Fits the Bill	168
I Told You, But Did I Show You?	169
Choosing the Season	170
Older But Not Wiser	171

Contrarian's Cure	172
Solar Maximum	173
Identity Crisis	174
Fluid Constructs	175
Wrapped in Cellophane	176
Terrarium Prisoner	177
Zip Code Comparisons	178
Sunset Pairings	179
A Soft Remembrance	180
Cycle of Be-Longing	181
Millennia with a Mercurial Babysitter	182
Thriving Quietly, Without Rain	183
Warm Waters on My Cheeks	184
Return to Sender	185
More Habit than Mere Sadness	186
Dawning of a New Melody	187
The Sound of Surrender	188
Defaced	189
Final Cut	190
Final Tribute	191
Tidal Reverence	192
Acknowledgements	193
About the Author	195

I can only write in the after—
questions spilled, the hurt culled,
when blood rushes back to my fingers,
tingling after frostbite.

Prologue

What do you heal from?
Who do you heal for?

I heal for the short, budding flower,
cut too soon, discarded.

I heal for the little girl who slipped,
cried so hard, she couldn't breathe.

I heal for the child's mother,
broom-haired, onion-sleeved—

calling from across the street
at a hollow in the dusk.

I heal for that gash in Earth's chest,
torn by the rub, riven by the subtle sting of love.

I heal for the angel raised by demons,
twice blind to the light he couldn't take.

I heal for those who cannot heal,
for those who cannot hear their own heart break.

Evergreen Fandango

One clear night, then three gray days.
Sharp rain shatters against the frigid earth—
a flash fandango. This quasi-gloom
thumps between my temples:
feet and tambourines, guitars and castanets—
their beat pounds in this quiet temple.

I wish I spoke your language
of deciduous fondness. I've always been
a loyal, boring evergreen, at home
in the tropics, or summering in the Sierras.
My needles dull at times,
but they hardly ever fall.

Everything else changes, while I remain
a taller version of what I was:
roots in the earth, manicured boughs,
not taking up too much space—
lest I constrain the other who likes to spread
their arms far and wide, or dare
to step forward and dance my own fandango.

Rewind

The leaves unfall, ascending
back to the tree
where they unblush, unthink
what you whispered in their ears.
Then, they ungrow, undrinking
the earth's saccharine tears
and unwind back to the field
of possibility where you grow
from a tiny, boundless spark
of the all, pulsing with glee,
dying to be born.

Forging Light

Swallows peck at the expanse
once brimming with your presence.
Turbid puddles lie still,
charcoal craters within my grasp.
I anoint my face with mud,
and let it dry me.

I merge into traffic
with the mob of shadows.
We sway in unison, a silent trance.
I carve yet another hollow
with my mulish feet,
morph into an effigy.

With my index finger, I trace
your old imprints in the void,
seeing the molds you once cast.
The crowd propels me onward.
I rub my arms like sticks,
undaunted by the impending storm.

The desert's mouth cracks open,
the assembly hushes, inert.
Sparks burst like playful sprites.
I rise through the fire, claiming my place.
Where were you when I needed light?
Bound in chaos, I surmise.

Forward

Why do I have you,
subtle stain on my ruffled sleeve,
stones dragged by my skirt
of endless anguish—
sighs that do not shift,
backward or toward infinity,
space filled with excess air
we do not share?

Why do I stare at you
when I don't remember you,
if the strokes of your polished eyebrows
blend with winter,
If I lose myself at the crossroads
of your outstretched arms
(reaching inward, never toward me)?

Why would I tell you
about this irreverent oblivion
that trenches and limps,
stacking lives in the keeping room,
where you wait for me, seated,
as though I were to appear—
as if the firm hand of kindness
had not thrust me, furiously
and against my will, forward?

Eden

I know you existed beyond waves of farewell
on a faded canvas, yielding to the drunken sand
in frothy genuflection.

We were the children in the backstory,
giants under the gilded sun.
Elephants atop the hill, evident to all,
save our innocent eyes; crushing peaches
underfoot, in gleeful sealed-eye tantrums,
our stomachs growling familiar tunes.
We were the melody of the cherubim,
home's highest frequency recalled by tears.

What do we really know of love?
Let's not speak of it while we tread this garden.
Lest we step on the exposed roots of an ancient,
one-legged feeling, leaning on a cane,
dragging wrinkled feet over fresh turf—
lost in bygone whispers,
where laughter once pierced the air.

There are no colors here to depict our memories,
but I have seen you, pure and vivid,
speaking my language wordlessly,
grasping my hand, unasked, guiding me
through dying orchards to the embracing meadow.

Desert Stones

I felt you
in the dry cough of the ailing desert,
suspended between dust and breath,
just another morning.

I found you,
torn between pine and thorn,
where my feet no longer tread,
amid the boulders.

I saw you
in the blush of demure rocks,
warm and bare
before a sentient canyon.

I asked you
to rise with me
in a chant of deep sighs,
and learn the Sun's precepts.

I wept for you,
dry-faced
in the improbable farewell
of a timid gloaming,
saving my tears
for the impending thirst.

A Silent Banquet

I shy away from the sun. The world claims
blank plaques, stripeless ribbons with faux
gold medallions, featureless faces blurred
by fate's scorching hand.

Here I don't reside, wary of the impending
morrow, or the capricious birds, devouring
seeds I gave them dangling from a feeder,
within my sight's very brawn.

Within this symphony, a tranquil, gentle strand.
No smoke shall daunt the wasps who indulge
in my grapes, bursting upon boughs
in a southern landscape.

Their mercurial ripeness, taunting my gaze,
with an almost blue of sweetness, a sour Bordeaux,
and a stillborn green that neither fades nor grows.

I won't shoo them away. They are here
for my banquet, for they too can hear the beat
of the entrancing drums echoing like chants
within the earth's languid womb.

With two cautious fingers, I pluck a grape
while the zealous sun whips my neck.
My pudgy nose boils and my cheeks simmer

with a feverish joy.

My mouth, an acid and saccharine frisson,
I nearly ingest the notion with two leery seeds.
Would they take root within me?
I expel the skin after drawing out its bloom.

crickets own the night
the beaver moon is silent
I shush my loud heart

Sacrificial Lamb

I grab the pencil and hesitate
to write you alive,
for your lips in mine never were
an intellectual exercise.
Paper tires of futile words.
How many trees shall be
sacrificed to this love?
I still don't know how to sketch
the faintest, faithful outline
of your face in the daylight.

Undercurrent

Embox this secret.
The livid ocean makes no sound
as it beats against dead coral.
Hot air pushes north—
the fury of a storm.
Silence that is neither
eloquent nor mysterious.
I've known you beneath the waves,
beyond the ripples of a breath
too deep to measure,
too dense to hold.

Play Dough

It swells, it smirks—
this cotton-candy silence.
It melts in my mouth
of simmering yesterdays.
I chase tomorrow's wisp
(nutmeg and rising flour),
break it to inhale your hands
in the dough. Your gazpacho eyes,
a cool retreat from this endless summer.

Tidal Draw

Your hands irk with sand—
a zillion crystals skyscrape
your fingertips.
You beam at the sparkling castle
of packable ground quartz.

Here in the forest, trees stand dry.
Gazes pinball from crown to branch.
Owls glisten at the switch of night.
Silence befalls me, and I crumble
under your tide.

The Pail of Whispers

Every whisper has a pail, waiting,
its ears perched high on the hill's crest.
How did I get here without you?
This sacred litany of molten echoes.
I digress.

The pail of whispers, heavy
and brooding by the waterfalls.
I approach or step away
with feet reversed like a *Ciguapa*[1].

If I ever reach it, I may know
why climbing's righteous but lying is not,
why magnolias take their time
to stain sidewalks with their stubbornness—

why the voice that whispers near
is never talking to me.

---

[1] Ciguapa: mythological creature in Dominican folklore, a woman with long hair, brown skin and backward-facing feet.

Pixelated Embrace

It's the fourth cigarette of an early evening.
Latin ballads drown out obscure poets
declaiming on tiny screens. This is life now,
an evening *tertulia* with her sister, miles away;
a pixelated embrace through a hovering cloud.

Who else, knowing her, will seize the moon
by its small waist, and walk hand in hand with her
toward the gates of slumber? Cups brim with
endless musings, reminiscing for its own sake,
as if to season the insipid present with the profane.

Eons ago, before school bells and smartphones,
at 3:00 a.m., the night was still young,
and hopeful yuppies crowded the Atlantic Cafe.
Girls feigned indifference to finger-twirling;
beer-emboldened young men vied for a spin
on the tile dance floor.

Tonight, she shuffles a concert of songs, singing
verses she could have written of bygone lovers,
forgotten dreams, and sipping rum.
She dilutes the euphoria with ice,
but rum does not curb the chill of winter,
nor is it a lasting tonic for an aching void.

Subtle Victory

Dandelion, you break me
into translucent sighs
of a bygone August, prancing
lithely, free from qualms
too far from home.

Espadrille steps, unheard
on the parched grass.
You're concealed from sight—
except to those who don't
look down on you,

for you've already won.
You fell apart,
scattering seeds like wishes—
an ancient art—
adrift with possibility
where others die.

For Lily[2]

She lies still, her petals tucked in,
an inward blossom no one should see,
lest she wilt, lest her hues be deemed
not of this world. Lest the hand
pointing downward on her heart, flip back,
reaching for a wish not hers to grasp.

He plants lilies under the treehouse
where they first drank a honey sky,
licking the raw off each other's fingers.
Bees gallivant from linden to lavender,
to the sweet clover of her voice.

Mesmerized, she sees him as if
for the first time. "I sleep soundly, my love,
below our makeshift shelter, snug
in the bosom of a recurring dream,
free to be me in a wide bed of roots—
kissed softly and wrapped tightly
in my cello's velvet threnody."

---

[2] Inspired by the book *Mad Honey*

Gangrene

Dead tissue, blackened fragments of you
fall, gangrened. Yesterday, when you lived,
worlds spun in your head faster than you
could utter them.

Today, you hunger for a hug (the kind
you seldom got), but no one turns
when you attempt a word. Only ghosts
open their arms to you.

Their dementor robes agape, undulating,
crack the static. You can see the smile
on their featureless faces. One of them
beckons you when a wisp of warmth
envelops their hollowness.

You walk to them, for the first time since
monolith skies collapsed into a wheelchair.

Your body fills with mirth and light.
Your polished lips curl upward.
A Great Wall[3] fades into peach blossoms.
You find their hand: a friend at last!

---

[3] In memoriam: W.W.

To the IKEA Mannequin on My Shelf

Little man, raise one leg
and the Earth will levitate
away from its bosom.
Her dainty damsel spirit
distills the day, fans her face
and gives me a wave.

Lift your arms, little man,
so trees can blossom.
I will place the bouquet
in your open hands.
Prime the land so I can create.

Dance on tiptoes, little man.
Leap away!
I will twirl in your place,
I will play your chimes,
and buy more time
for you to erase.

Blur the oceans, little man,
scratch the clouds.
I will find new ways
to depict the sky.
Uncork the stars
over the ocean's mane.

Shifting Eyes

If I tilt my head just so,
life may taste sweeter.
I might spot the good side
of the rotting persimmon,
burst its treacly flesh
with my bare teeth—

smear my face in shame,
ask for a drink
to rinse away my thirst,
the kind that stings
when you're nothing
but wounds.

I might notice the orchard
with good apples just beyond,
waiting to be picked.

Out There, the World

Early morning autumn,
with the bashful sun,
and a subliminal breeze
of continuity.

This isn't just another fall,
though the leaves may argue.
They've already blushed at the sight
of your shape in the dawn.

Your clear eyes hush the thunder
of a world now lost, a distant beacon
I don't rush toward,
despite being drawn.

Yet I know you're there,
quietly reminding me
of all that is just.

Liquid Suspension

Tripping on a rotting branch,
I climb into cyclic bowers
of a humid shadow, a place
that feels so much like home.

My friends are here.
The proverbial serpent
coils around my ankle.
My cat sleeps.
My bed: a cradle of moss,
and plush, wet leaves.

The forbidden apple tree
stands beside me.
I am free
to walk toward the radiance
calling beyond—but I don't.

I linger, stretching
in the quiet Eden
of this perpetual womb—
unborn.

Doom's Overture

A fairy amidst the rubble
spins her sunset dust
onto another bruised child
searching for their mom.
Wingless, gray butterflies
climb crumbling concrete walls,
like roaches drawing color
from the blood moon.

Though deaf and mute,
I hear the rumblings...
booted feet on desert runways,
startled laughing doves taking
to the sky. They, too, must take flight.
The pendulum swings 'yes'
when I ask, "Is this the end?"

But it is wrong. It is only dawn,
and we're barely awake.
I hear the choppers,
the screams, the bombs.
I hear the great tit sing,
pursued by sparrowhawks.
The crowded theater leans in,
and the curtain unfurls.

I Always Come Up Empty

Like miners, we pan
for the moment
when the cheerless sky
trauma bonds with the
butterscotch horizon.
I see you, lifetimes away,
beside me, and my belly growls.
I swallow a whale of longing,
diving into the passive,
massive past, sifting for
your slipping silhouette—
to catch my breath.

Sepia Stains

My once rufous lips,
now stained in sepia,
by the spatter of listless years...
Release my face,
etched within the boughs
of a slow unraveling.

My eyes fall like thunder
on shrinking roots,
in the wake of my tears.
I crumble slowly,
as I dry and meld into shallow bark.
The tree is dew-dampened
with dim desires.

I peel away after nightfall,
(face, fingers, limbs, and spine)
awash in the nocturnal hush.
Years gleam like rings
beneath my thinning skin.

Moonlit flowers bloom
from the weary springs of my eyes,
casting their ethereal glow.
Luna smiles a gentle, cool beam
upon my shoulders as I bid goodbye.

mountains crack their back—
pines chaperone lonely hills
I let love happen

Cataclysm

Breathless, pyroclastic flow
stills this hunger.

We drink from lidless vessels,
the restless spurts of
a stirring fever.

Besotted.

A fossil of a moment
that never was. Nothing lasts
when touched with such ardor.

No roof can hold steady
beneath the scalding ash.

Where Did the Clouds Go?

There is nowhere to hide.
As he notices me, the sun
lays an arm over my bare
forehead. Mountains burn
tangerine and marmalade
over my hair. He crowns me,
air and bourdeaux
and permeates my thoughts.
I am dry. I'm exposed.
I am emptied in his glow.

Hispaniola

The ocean grabs the island
by her palms and slaps both
her cheeks. One is blushed
hibiscus and molasses,
torrents of tempting thrills
making their way north.
Mountains sway arm in arm
from coast to coast.
The other cheek is bruised,
swollen with mighty strength,
tired of throwing tantrums
to the heedless night
that never ends.

Petals and Stars

One day,
I will pet the cosmos
as it wags its tail
outside my window,

take a deep inhale
when its petals reach
the unspoken divide.
I will survey its conquests

to the browning pine,
peel the ocean off my feet,
and forever wander barefoot
on the magnificent mile.

Harmonies

The wind soft-plucks my strings,
and I am music and bellflower dew.
Aflutter melodies reach out to me.

A jolt, a drumming, a skip...

Doors revolve around the seasons,
blooming shivering dreams.
Swollen earth and lively streams
flow within me in anticipation.

Flowing with the Stream

The surging rapids slowed.
The raging water ceased slapping
against unmoving boulders.

No salmon will leap upstream anymore.
Why fight the current?

Only a trickle remains,
barely wetting unbothered pebbles,
evanescing in the sun without closure.

Sometimes We Die

so a blue jay may
tap a lonely window
closer to spring,
so they can feel us

in a ray of sunshine
fondling their skin;
to whisper our truth
in someone's bad ear,

and finally hear that song
we often hummed but didn't know,
to become one, at last
with all that we cherish.

Release Me

Waters parted in his eyes
last time I saw him.
I tread on damp sands,
rushed by turbulent blues.
Amidst the surging waves,
I somehow escaped drowning,
reaching the wilderness
between his furrowed brows.
He seems distant, as if
trying to blink me out.
I just want to ride
his tears to freedom.

Shallow Grave

He stood impervious
to the gentle drizzle
soaking his bare chest.
Her eyes had browned
in clear places.

She treasured Earth
for its tenacity, for tulips
that bloom an inch
from the ground
without a catalyst—

buds that fracture the soil
with quiet vulnerability,
hands unclenched, unfolding,
fingers stretching toward the horizon,
to the very nadir of hope.

He once was strength,
unyielding and untamed,
defiant winds mocking tempests
gathered like blooms in a vase,
displayed for all to see.

Now, he stands exposed,
tears mingling with rain,
laid to rest amidst the bulbs.

Within

An orchid on the brink,
the telltale blush
of a suppressed wink.
I teeter on the curves
of an unsent love note,
and slip on black ink.
The dimout zooms in.
You will never hear
that last petal fall.
It's too loud within.

Inertia

Not now. It is not the time
to gaze upon the metal clock.
My eyes are still unfocused,
attuned to the swell within.
He's out there somewhere,
clamoring to the wind—rumbling
like thunder in my sleep.

The rain feels distant from me,
a vestige of memory, pattering
faintly on the glass. Yet here I sit,
water pooling past my ankles;
I need no sound to confirm
my drowning.

Well-trained bones know how
to move away from this, but I remain,
drifting with the unripe now.
My heart has shrunk,
though not as you may think.
It floats, minuscule, in this mason jar
of a moment, no denser for the tears.

It folds in deep stasis, buoyed.
For I can't weep this joy,
I can't crack this peace. I will not
shatter this silence into fragments.

Dharma

Should beauty percolate,
unseen and unheard,
and mend the rifts
of a fractured world...

Should love bind like gold
this broken, baked bowl
of scattered manna...

Should my words
ease the wheeze,
discordant to the wind
that strikes and blows,
I've done my job.

Portrait of a Missing Kiss

In your nymphalid silhouette,
organza wings, traced with dry crayon,
quiver before your gaze.

Sunken canyons of night slumber
in your eyes, captured and resigned.
On your lips, silence falters,

and within their creases, orchids thrive.
Thoughts dissolve, inadequate,
in the caldera of your mouth.

Blue jays burst through the locked gate
of your throat, and madness springs,
bewildered, in melodic notes.

padded snow blanket
tulips sweat under its warmth—
time to uncover

Hollow Ritual

Watch   for things   that   beg
for eyes,   when the   sentence   of a life
has reached   a period.
You don't follow   the words;
my words   follow you.
There is no meaning   to be drawn
from this hollow ritual.   Silence
tiptoes in the creek, but   it still   makes a noise.
There is no withdrawing   an armada   of tears.
They've already abraded   the rocks,   so no
sharp edges   may scratch your hands
when   you   hold them.

Brisk Awakening

Winter nears—all the excess fabric
clings to my limbs, soaked by wounds
I long deemed healed.

That faux warmth lulls me to sleep,
but the outer chill slaps me awake,
reminding me I can't go on living this way.

No more dreams, no more
weaving wistful strings—
shielding skin from bygone winds;
no more waiting for tranquil summers
to tear off scabs, as I shed the coat.

Neptune's Womb

Neptune-blue, this otherworldly creature—
an empty womb brought to term.
A hollow birth of jumbled murmurs
iterated for their own sake.

This vacant tomb does not echo.
You lie in your armor of crumpled leaves,
seeking no repose from the ongoing fall.
How many pleas can you shout into a void,
and still call it dialogue?

Meaning eddies, turbid, in this thallium pool.
It spirals and devolves into itself.
You're alone, growing organs and limbs
until your fingers are long enough
to point (accusingly) at your mother's heart.

You exist only in her eyes—no one else's—
absorbing the spoils of her bloodline,
her penchant for delusion and pinot noir.
A venomous ambrosia ribbons
from your navel to her anguish,
as you expand, immortal, in her incubator.

Winter's Touch

Blue winter crepes hang
from my cold shoulder blouse.
I peel myself off
the floral background,
clinging to the anonymous
distance of the glue-shedding sky;
my face, a collage of coltish blooms
bruised by a vengeful frost
that only wants to be accepted.

Lilith's Mark

Pondering your face
in the golden hour,
forsaken mist clouds your irises
when moonlight lingers
on your mother's sins
of omission and commission.

I never met the woman, but I am
a debtor to her credit, charged
for what she pilfered. As we all are,
in your eyes, the unyielding,
softer kind. Alluring succubi
of a ruthless goddess, calderas that
beckon, untouched and untouchable,
for caressing them foolishly
courts disfigurement.

I pretend you exist,
even in the dearth of proof.
A phantom carries weight and mass
when one craves a presence:
a warm wisp over my shoulder,
a humid towel I never used,
an education *in absentia*,
your fleeting spectral in my sheets,
an ethereal calumny,
recounting ways I've erred.

I am not real either, yet I race
unrestrained through the parched
vastness of your nights,
guilty as charged—your eluded
and inevitable demise.

golden beach sojourn
Saharan dust on my curls
I, too, get to shine

Once a Mermaid

Saharan dust settles on my curls,
like glitter on glue. I shimmer
for all the wrong reasons
on this golden beach. The sun hides
behind a beige blanket of sky.
Cool water rebels against my thighs.
This nightmare of pushing against
the waves, rough years crashing
under their own weight.
I retreat to the sea,
my turquoise tail turning upward.
Maybe I wasn't meant for legs,
I gather—gills seething,
wet arms reaching toward Atlantis.

Thanksgiving

I unravel the tale of a leaf aboard the morning
train. Today is the eve—she must brave
the homeward odyssey. The Southern sky,
no less solemn in its mildness, casts its torpor
over the rain.

I kindle a furnace, a modest flame within my chest,
once defiant, now an act of gratitude. I splash
a handful of pristine words over my face, gazing
into the mirror at the concave world.

Tomorrow, I'll bake a ham and a turkey breast—
whipping tradition in a nest of migratory birds.
My door will open to those I don't fully know,
for some people remain unknowable.

They'll speak my language through a crystal wall.
I will watch their lips move, their tongues curve,
but the chisel shaping their thoughts will stay
unseen.

Still, we'll oblige, converse on our shared bounty, a
common ground affirmed over a mouthful of
pumpkin pie.

Through Broken Gates

We make a home from ancient ruins,
rebuild crumbling arches
to frame our silhouettes.

Windows have no glass;
storms don't visit the Field of Reeds.
You stand by the fallen gate—

rusted iron, and hard-wired fondness.
Your dry, calloused hands
have loosened our hardened moments.

You wink—affirmed irrationality...
I follow you to the very edge,
stacking bricks over the mystery.

Belated Thanks

I once shattered and mended
beneath your lips.
You tore the violet night asunder
and stitched me a quilt.
I slept... lifetimes in your bed,
cradled by feathers and silk.

You greeted the gleaming dawn
with a tip of your hat.
You made no sound.
I had yet to wake up.
I never thanked you for sheltering me
from the rain as you left,
leaving the umbrella in my grasp.

pine cones and tree lights
a lonely child's Christmas wish
twinkles in the night

Christmas in Quisqueya

A plane's descent places me in a distinct timeline. The mild Caribbean zephyr, palms clapping in welcome as they witness my landing. I can always come home, they remark, unsolicited, a comforting truth.

The sea, a constant, lies still in its implausible azure grotto. Each drop of aquarelle deepens its temperance until a pulsing singularity broods beneath, observant. My eyes pour into its vastness, a family reunion.

Come Christmas Eve, we'll enjoy a feast: a roasted piglet, plantain pockets snug in banana leaves, elbow and potato salad, savory rice with pigeon peas, chilled beer for the elders, merengue soda for the kids.

History won't recount this. These soulful chronicles belong to poets and priests. Yet every islander is an aphorist, a philosopher, a sentient tome of island lore, a coconut shell for a spine—a motley bloodline congealed in amber, high on the crests of earthbound sentinels, indecipherable from the shore.

I embrace myself in my mother's arms and rediscover my missing spark in the jovial irises of my siblings' eyes.

Two Dolls and Three Kings

I only ever owned two dolls, delicate treasures in a world where Barbies belonged to children with ties to distant lands like the United States or, in a bygone era, Venezuela.

My dolls weren't the coveted reborn dolls of the '80s, the ones I daydreamed about swaddling and adorning with miniature outfits like real infants. No, my dolls were not my first choice, but they were unique—a second-hand, silicone-skinned Japanese doll with straight chestnut hair, a miniature yogi ready to bend and twist to my whims. The other, a robust, plastic blonde doll with pigtail braids, remained shelved most of the time, but I could never forget her.

How did I come to possess a Japanese doll while living in the insular mountains of the 1980s Dominican Republic? My recollection is hazy, but I remember it as a gift from a Spanish missionary whom my family hosted one summer while she worked with the church. The doll had meager clothes, so I fashioned her an outfit with fabric scraps and my rudimentary sewing skills.

The blonde doll had been a "Three Kings" gift from my dad. Christmas gifts were for Americans.

Dominican kids didn't have Santa. We had the Three Kings, who somehow made no noise as they filled our rooms with their camels on the eve of January 6th, delivering our toys. Oh, coveted joy! They were the only gifts of the year for many of us. "At least you had toys," my siblings would chime in. But this isn't a sad story about growing up in a small town in the countryside of a humble island. This isn't a sad story at all.

Sure, we had limited means, but we never lacked what truly mattered: a roof of our own, honest and loving parents, friends galore, and a multitude of cousins. Cousins to play hide and seek with, tackle homework with, attend church together, and, of course, get into the occasional trouble with. And then there were the lush mountains, always smiling around me, offering endless adventures and mysteries. Our home had no television when I was a kid, and it wasn't until I reached my teenage years that we got a fridge. Bicycles or scooters were scarce, and cars? They were a luxury reserved solely for the 'rich,' although even those we deemed 'rich' carried their own burdens—a spouse who had migrated to the United States, the trials of managing a small-town business, or concealed guilt.

No, I never felt poor. We had what we needed and nothing more, except for food. Come what may, we had food—for everyone at home, for the neighbor who couldn't afford to cook, for my grandpa who preferred my mom's cooking, though he didn't live with us, for the occasional country visitor, my father's third cousin, or the Haitian woman with a child who stopped by every few months. I couldn't remember her name or whether she had a home. There was always plenty of food, even if my mom had to make herself a meal from our leftovers. But this isn't a sad story, no.

This is a tale of devotion—a father who wanted to give me the childhood he never had growing up as a farmer's kid in the mountains of Camú.

One evening, approaching January 6th, I witnessed a secret ritual. My late father, convinced I was asleep, concealed a grand, plastic doll within a duffle bag hanging from a nail on the wooden wall, believing he had hidden it where I would never think to look. I smiled and turned sideways, pretending to be asleep.

Outside, the usual chorus of crickets remained silent. The unsightly toads in the nearby miniature swamp, where taro root and yautía malanga thrived unbidden yet embraced, also remained silent. Nor did I hear a whisper from the brown geckos that crept about our small-town dwelling, which we regarded as an auspicious omen.

The next day, I didn't say a word, filled with excitement as I eagerly awaited the surprise at the foot of my bed on Three Kings' Day. I remained silent because, more than a toy, I cherished the joy of my father's belief in magic.

The Art of Unbinding

I reside in the moment when the sun highlights my back, and a tower of eagles stacks its glee upon my shoulders. The streets decelerate and undulate in slow motion until they freeze on the canvas of a scarlet cocktail dress. You linger in a corner, smudged in drizzle. I kiss you and kiss you until we wake up.

I unscrew my diamond earrings, the ones I never sleep without. They've left celestial imprints on my earlobes, two stars etched in the flesh. It's time for new studs, ones that don't claim a piece of me. I've left too much skin on dreams I can't recall. Tonight, I wash my silk down comforter. Sweat and tears rush from the washing machine, purging both fabric and home. A new dwelling, for I have yet to name this feeling.

Some of us like to sculpt beyond the marked horizon. We wear the gratuitous daisy, fixed high upon our tresses. We harbor the ironic giggle deep within our lungs. We see the stardust pulsing under unmoving boulders. We recognize the angel and the demon on our shoulders, and let whispers of their voices fade, as we carve our will on the distant hills, far from the confines of reason.

I love you. I hope that much is clear. You won't doubt me at this point, for we have awakened each other in far too many worlds from a smudged, wintry dream. I have grown beyond my skin, far past my aura of malaise and admonition. I am not ashamed of this hope, grinning like a pansy in the chill. No, there is no shadow of remorse in my smirk.

Mindfulness

Prettier than a primrose blooming in the desert,
more soothing than a sunset over a sleepy sea,
softer than the snow stalling frigid mornings,
more fragile than happiness, her crystal hands.

If you lift them to the sky, they exude divinity.
Point them to the forest, she reveals pine.
Aim them at the soil, she'll cleave it open
so you can see your own fault lines.

A sensuous moonlit whisper, her gentle laughter,
a melody weaving through the quiet night.
Mystic as the sea, her eyes will draw you,
a universe spinning in a placid trance.

If you embrace her in the shadows' tender hold,
you will find serenity, as new paths unfold.

violets in winter
mouths open, slowly sipping
the tepid sun

Holly

Fleeing the balmy wind, you alight,
pumpkin-breasted and blue-winged,
in the open mouth of a scrub holly.
Light-footed, you squeeze between
crimson berries and toothed leaves.

Why brave its impenetrable boughs
on a clear day? Denying wholeness,
shuffling fragments within, you hide
from cloudless skies in search of a seed.
Here's my feeder; have your fill of all
you resent me for. The hunger that won't leave
when I close, like a modest moonflower.

Tonight, I unveil my innocence,
and you will watch, as usual,
from your higher roost. Ever swollen,
your mighty chest, scarlet
from the sting of rustling leaves.

Little Mercies

You turn away.
A dense curtain of wind
sweeps before me;
I can't see your back.
I can't hear your voice
beyond its mocking howl:

Behold the loss.
Feel its draconian press
upon your chest,
and carry it stoically
toward unspent tomorrows.

Pinecone Vernacular

My personal sun now perches
upon another's vertex.
My crown has dulled,
shifting from vibrant gold
to an aged bronze.

Yet this pinecone fountain flows
ever upward, as does yours.
This is our vernacular, spoken softly
through screens and walls.

We shall hear our song
beyond the murmurs of a chatterbox
that hides when observed.

Live—just one more day, every day.
Tomorrow, we shall split a star,
dipped in café au lait
on a Parisian street.

We will dive and breach the horizon,
like swordfish in the Caribbean Sea.
We'll slice the water in half,
proudly peering beyond the abyss.

The Forgotten Snow

Art speaks to me in garbled sentences—
static nonbeings in overheard soliloquies,
like this winter landscape painted by a child
yearning for the absent snow.

I won't return to that spurious scenery,
where snowmen moonwalk the day, galvanized
by the wind, complete with carrots and sticks,
their noses gentler than their trunks, for it is
bitterly, bitterly cold beneath their holly hats.

I won't rescue you this time.
You will melt with the gleaming snow,
before the faithful watch of Noble Firs.
I am not yet in my element,
but I jog the southbound track.
These vernal fogs gagging the sky are still foreign.
Yet, I cover my skin as I long for summer—
sundresses and linen nodding at the sun.

I can linger in this liminal loft,
preserving garden crops,
wandering unknown lands aglow in a book,
stretching my limbs to see how much I've grown,
teaching my child how to forget
the plush, immaculate snow.

Soul Soaking

The tiny Christmas tree is propped on the shelf. Below it, clad in red, sits the mischievous elf. It's nearly February; might as well wait to celebrate the Lunar New Year, squeeze a bit more light out of the twinkling tree.

Days knock at my door, asking if we can go out. Dysania visible, my answer is the same: Not yet, I'm fatigued. Dishes to wash, meals to cook, ennui to iron on high until the steam blushes my cheeks.

The thirsty plants agree, it's not yet time; they need water and food, as do my fears. The stacks of books on the high shelf concur I mustn't go anywhere. Stories to read, poems to write, ever waiting for a chronic longing to subside.

The laundry yells from afar, you have dismay to dry, stained whites to soak in a vinegar mixture of hopes.

No! interject my thoughts: there is much thinking to do about all you need to do and everything you didn't do. The random beat of my pores bursts and screams last: Remember... YOU.

Elegy of a Passing Wish

If nostalgia threatened
to exhume my bones,
already melded with the quartz
of a forsaken shore,
tell it no. Let me rest,
cradled in salt, absorbed
by the hush of the subtle sand—
unnamable and ineffable
among its grains,
swept by the waves,
like the velleity I was.

Borrowed Time

She lives on an island she's never ventured beyond, and the ocean remains a distant mystery. Perched high in a valley among giants, she sits amidst palms, eggplant, and banana leaves, wrapped in wrinkles and fleece. Beside her rests a burlap sack brimming with spiky, green annatto pods in their heart-shaped glory. Behind her, a red achiote (Bija) tree flourishes, invoking memories of *mamá* (my grandmother).

I picture the vermillion-striped faces of her *Taíno* ancestors, and my mother, infusing her Spanish rice with the prized ground bija seeds, as saffron is absent from Hispaniola. It's winter in the sky-soaked mountains of Manabao, and the days are brief. This is not the coastal Dominican Republic in the travel brochures.

The sun has etched her unguarded face for over nine decades, leaving behind brown spots, a frozen frown, and brittle skin. Yet today, its warmth barely caresses the ground before ascending skyward in a perplexed mid-afternoon haze. So, she sits, puffing the pipe she's smoked since age ten, with tobacco that sprouted from the same land that witnessed her birth and that of her children, the land where my mother picked coffee beans, and learned of chaperoned love, under the watchful eyes of tradition.

She is my oldest maternal aunt, and I can see my grandfather in her fragile but self-assured countenance. She grins at me, her blue eyes incongruent with the inland greenery, and admits she's on borrowed time, in no rush to settle her debt.

When You Return

Dragonfly, wounded wing in flight,
darting to sunlit spots—
gallivanting gossamer gliders
that mimic the march of time.
By this tranquil pool, I lie,
taken by your flitting dance.

Will you return once winter is gone?
I'll save you a feast of flies and gnats—
a homemade banquet all summer long,
neatly arranged by the tomato patch.
A bed of perky daisies shall be yours,
a soft landing for your lithe form.

Urgency of the Unhealed

You return, a wrecking ball
in the night, knocking over objects,
stumbling in your plight.
You reach my bed. A crimson trail
shines behind your bare feet.
"See me!" you scream, unawakened
and unhealed, in ragged clothes,
wearing pain like an insignia.
This isn't you. I refuse to look.
Strip away the stiff facade
into the cleansing nook.
Bathe away the crusty anguish,
scrub the hardwood floors.
I'll wait for you, unsullied,
beyond these glass doors.

Untapped Shores

With subtle force, the sea snaps and lashes
at the weathered coral of history, scraping away
the slime clinging to the browned stone.
It screeches a strident anthem of strength,
both familiar and elusive. At night, it seeps into a
lullaby, unheard amidst the white noise monotone.

The sea forms a natural pool, though you wouldn't
know it now that it's livid. In its calm moments,
you can see fish, anemone, and peering eyes,
sirens beckoning you to their depths.
Sun-sliced hair appears green under the waves
of change, and hearts beat steadily under short-
sleeved, linen garments.

This is the home I don't yet know, a nagging
yet sweet hiraeth. My dreams sparkle, untapped,
under its vast, emerald blue.
Could it be that I can't swim, that my lungs fall
short of breath to advance unaided? Could it be
that I have many lives, and one is yet to unfold
under the fury of this wave?

Head Stand

My head on the ground,
Earth flattens my crown,
balancing on a tender point.
Now, fingertips massage the grass,
verdant blades camouflage her pain.
But I know my feet have stomped
on places they shouldn't have,
so I lift them with my legs.
She's a bit less sore now,
that I am upside down.

Power Play

His wrinkled, sweaty hands are heavy
as he kneads my frozen shoulders.

"Do you like this?" he asks.
"Not one bit," I reply.

Slowing down, displeased,
he retracts his hands. Then, he walks
into his friend's office: my boss's boss.
I keep typing while I sigh.

A few weeks later, it's just me and him
in the elevator. *What will he do this time?*
I grow a bit taller on my four-inch heels,
my lips form a disapproving pout.

"You should always wear red on those lips."
He orders. "They are meant to stand out."

I lift my chin and look away.
Never show fear when you're the prey.

I stretch my thighs
from derrière to amber coast
a seagull soars

More than Skin

It's not my body you miss,
now that I have turned to ash
over the crispy leaves.

It's not my voice you wish to hear
before you awaken on the other side—
a place where I'm also absent.

It makes you wonder if you made me up.
It's not my breath that warms your neck,
like a friendly ghost by a dying fire.

It's the moonflower in your chest,
blooming immaculately without sun,
unpluckable, yet plush to the touch.

It's the down that filled your eyes—
donning the pulchritude
of a snowy morning...

the supernova of your speeding heart
rushing outward—spilling—
like clear water over a full cup.

Conjuring Beauty

You can summon beauty
like one calls a bird.
Hang a bird feeder
and patiently wait.

Soon, fiery cardinals
will thaw the frigid day.
Place the feeder where
you can see them play.

Sit under a blanket
by the light-framed glass.
Behind you, another fire,
tongues quavering in stoic silence,
wrapped in a blue aura.

Call it magic when the birds appear,
blue and crimson, gray and twilight.
Their wings, fleet and flutter
with your every blink, taking turns
to amaze you with their mere existence.

Sweet Mortality

The desert succumbs
in a rendezvous of rainfall.
The beach dissolves
in melancholia for the mountain.

The night expires
in the intransigence of the day—
newborn yet wise,
fragrant, and tender.

The void of possibility
meets its end.
Clouds linger in sobs
on the grieving sky.

The year withers in winter,
and within it, it revives—
wishful yet cautious,
hungover with hope.

And I die, moonstruck and enlivened
by an aureate glow.
An aura of mint and modesty
restrains the greed of the moment I find you—

coddled and caught,
outspread... in my voice.

Undeniable

And even more, I love you—
an endless replay
of a farewell at dawn.
You unwrinkle my hand
with a kiss
and deride the past
as a vexatious trial
of a present act.

This crime of holding you
hostage within my eyes,
as if in a leap, you couldn't
invade my fascia,
as if the sky were a corral
for the seraphim,
as if the rainbow went unnoticed
on a sunny, rainy day.

Screens and Shadows

You dwell amid the living,
a meme on someone's dimly lit screen.
You indulge your right to pleasure,
drenched in the damnable plasma of sensation.
Lost in a jungle of neurons and silicon,
astute fingers map your thighs.
Lightning flickers, the awakening forest sweats.
You fold forward, arms twisted in reverse prayer.
Unanswered longing seeps
into the parched earth, languid.

I live among the dead, a fragrant specter
of coffee stains and half-eaten pastries.
Pantries filled with mason jars,
time preserved as a souvenir,
for I need no nourishment.
Winter days camouflage me.
Mist rains invisibly
through the scarcely-leafed pines.
I know my exact location
in this place without landmarks.
Mornings smell like cinnamon and birdsong.
Afternoons flirt hopelessly with the aloof sun,
and vapid, condensed nights
fill the bottom of this empty bowl.

a yellow leaf falls
I wear my favorite color
past the naked tree

Molting the Rough

He thinks he knows me
because he saw me naked
before I shed my slough.
He wouldn't look beneath
the rough, youthful scales—
glazed in a candid, inner kiln.
Nor would he caress
the smoldering flesh,
stratified and simmering
with guileless impetus.

It's time to sand my muskmelon skin,
cracked by a mighty winter.
My life cleaves in slices,
each morsel sweet, ripened and
mellowed by an ageless softness.
Hardshell ridges will form again,
and once more, I shall polish them,
beneath a moonroof of pine—
awaiting the promised warmth.

Promised Land

If I knew you
beyond the robin's trill,
past the cricket's hum,
past the sage exhale
of a hollowed oak,

I knew you would return
behind the veil of a dappled sun,
draped in light—
moss and fern beading
from the humid dusk
of your ripened skin.

I would know your arms
as a holy highway
to the promised land,
nirvana as an enduring breath,
and your lips,
as the endgame of hope.

Yogi Freedom Ride

I lift my foot to my ear,
and ring my heart,
reminding it
that healing is a stop,
not the entire path.
Space unbinds
when I twist my spine.
Pain simmers
like sweet and sour jam
when I stretch my legs.

A doorless vessel
is a unique form of freedom—
freefall surrender
within every tender fold.
My chest tilts upwards
in wheel pose.
I can't be anywhere else
when in the deep grooves
of my pulsating blood.

Liminal Gaze

Bury me in your sepulcher
as my tired eyes yield
their last hint of light.
Let your steps on my soil
be the ultimate caress
before I journey across
the liminal frontier.
Idle, I'll be,
watching you dream
from a novel corner—
weighing your heart, at last,
with unseen hands.

Evil Eye

Bad days transcend mere bad luck;
they reach beyond simple melancholy.
There was a moment when restless shadows
aspired to break free from tethering at our feet,
idling near the sundial.

They abandoned us, merged with kindred forms.
Together, they roam senescent roads
and balter around strangers' homes,
often unbeknownst to us
and their unsuspecting hosts.

They don't return after a rain or flood;
they crave no sustenance from our sinking steps,
but we are far from alone. We remain, unaware,
in the unsettling embrace of another's shadow.

Drowning Weight

It all ends here,
six feet under a sigh—
deeper than the flooded basin
of eroded sadness.
It shimmers now,
with twilight's blush,
and the verdant brush
of stolen hope.
This concrete tongue,
heavier than my heart, sinks
beneath the accordion cries
of a chronic torpor—
a drowned goodbye.

Bewilderment of Moon

Three songs to love, and one to spite.
Moonwater sprinklers engorge
the thirsty broom sedge night.
Your voice, thundering,
shatters quietly in my valleys.

Rivers run backward, as they should,
when the clock has stopped and dares not tick.
Everything stops growing, but defiant roses,
defoliating the dull, frail seconds.

This world is, then, a blinding madness
of aimless petals, damp and shriveled,
suspended in the deep bowl of the ether—
orphaned, without a page of a book to dry on.

White-winged Serenade

We clutched the jetlagged dawn
a little tighter.
Our room, a sexy fishbowl
to the pecking White Cockatoo.
Tell me it wasn't sneering
at our dotty smiles
as we gazed beyond it
to the placid shore.
The randy tide, subdued
by the early morning embers,
poised to resurge.

What does it take to keep a soul alive?

A sip of sun, even lukewarm,
soaked through a bright window.

A vault of misremembered moments
waiting to be claimed.

A pinch of dust
on the sterile calm of a winter day.

The unmatched wisdom
of a dogma-free embrace.

A penance of silence between lives,
as requisite intermission.

Entanglements

I'm wedded to the whir
of silent streets,
to the capricious, gray mane
veiling the sky.
To the impassive countenance
of a loveless day,
to the emotions spilled
in twilight's battle-sweat[4],
to the composure of a fractal,
crawling to infinity,
to the irony of your love.

---

[4] Kenning - battle-sweat: blood

It Dawns and Redawns

When did I become
a sublimated sketch of a curve?
How did I forfeit the touch
and scent of my daring lover?
His docile hair entrapped
beneath a vented helmet
on a warm Friday evening,
the smitten breeze teasing
his smile. The moon, waxing
the apple crisp of our nights
with her envious, tenuous light.

How did I lose my way
in the straits of a smudged horizon—
his heavy hand over my shoulder,
his plush rug under my feet?
I stumble upon another velvet body
and forget it's him. It's always him,
hurrying to graze my lips
with homegrown grapes—
plump and perfumed, pigmenting
the feet of the sky above me.

I see him. I truly see him
in the grooves of his callous hands—
ones that aged, bittersweet,
holding mine.

Year of the Dragon

Forgotten, like sin in a faraway land,
the new moon malingers
behind the beaded curtains
of a new year.

I save myself, with unlit candles,
for a blackout day.
Dust pools on viscous wax
like a dubious premonition.

And I know no dragon
who would tempt their fate
in the hazy lakes
of your ashen firmament,

chasing its tail
in your reckless gyre,
spewing fire,
for lack of words.

Living for the Chase

Chimeras leap from murals,
glossy and plump, loitering
in the littered alleys of our minds.
We keep tracing spirals
with a worn, sable brush,
in the irredeemable emerald of hope.

Familiar footfalls disrupt our sleep.
We tread through would-be worlds—
our feet laden with dust,
our chests torn in a twist.

Shall we sleep, then, as the horizon
rinses its mouth with resignation?
Its face, a shepherd's delight,
its gaze, a picaresque wink
to flaws and failings.

I, too, at times, ride
the inveterate horse of regret,
only to fall, headfirst
on the bald spot of an unfazed earth.
Sore, I'm pulled toward the grace
of the growing forest teeming beyond.

Riding the Milky Way

Clouds fall, mouth agape.
There is more rain than sky.
Space beckons through Earth's
open sunroof, an abyssal magnet
emitting a perpetual hum.

I ascend, as does each violet petal
defying the cold. Higher we glide,
riding the tailwind
of a profound surrender.

How minuscule we are
inside this Great White Shark—
our screams, mere growls
bouncing in its vast belly.
Yet, somewhere, someone hears us,
tickling giggling daffodils
into an early bloom.

Broken Record

She watches others
read cards and speak in tongues,
snoozing and awakening
within the ceaseless
chrome wheel.

Turntable seconds
scratch her eyes for melodies,
yet she won't play.
She is now a broken record.

Sacrificed oaks
stand sentinel behind her,
cradling her books
with weathered hands,
holding her fragile,
blown crystal figurine.

Whispers of the Watershed

Mountains drink from emerald flasks,
easing the knot in the forest's heart.
Our feet steeped in mud, we plod on—
weary and ungrateful, dwarfed
by sage titans who knew their path
to love. Don't lament the warmth
that nestled gently beneath your bones
once I was gone. Don't cry for me.

For I am home, backstroking the lazy river
spread upon the earth's collarbone.
At times, I swim; at others, float—
one with the unyielding current.
It's not true that the one who opens wider
can hold more. I cradled a giant boulder
I couldn't see through or beyond.
Now I grasp the clarity of the stream
in my outstretched arms, as I let go.

Drafting the Improbable

Maybe I penned you into existence,
virile and polished in a mythical romance.

As distant as you could be,
as implausible as I could withstand.

My vibrant Antillean plumes, a lure
for your dewy, mainland eyes.

Their stellium of sorrow, a mandate
to my poised, mending lips.

My awkward hands, spilling ebony ink
across the white picket fence.

Your unsaid goodbye, darting to the brink
of a stained, weathered page.

Sulking with the Missing Bloom

What can I say to cheer you up
that you don't already know?
Spring approaches,
but her scent eludes me,
veiled behind oppressive clouds
in the sulking sky. Silent,
their siblings unaware
of the storms within.
Yet they all recognize
the patter of cold rain
over twin towers. Paths weave
from mouth to mouth, spreading
tales of the impending bloom
that never comes.

Limping Devils

Dissociation. Years lash my hips
like a *diablo cojuelo* at Carnival.
Their whip, a brusque awakening
(beware where you stand).

Adrift in a sea of onlookers,
watching limping devils shake
their grotesque heads, mesmerized
by the allure of their horrid costumes,
by the care taken to bejewel their horns.

My mother's caution rings in my left ear:
don't linger up front, where they can spot you,
vulnerable and exposed, light-skinned,
long legs in shorts, inviting a bruise
on a warm Sunday afternoon. Blend in
with the animated crowd. Shelter
under the canopy of their upbeat chant.

The entrancing beat of a familiar drum
leads the festivities. A triumphant trumpet
vies with the hurried beat of my heart.
This cacophonous, frantic world
I feel estranged from, where I long to be
shielded, staying safe by remaining unseen.

Offering

Sip from the singing bowl
of my empty palms, soft waters
from a far-off morrow.
I, the dry lacuna
of a dream that slipped—
subtle lines engraved
on the gleaming brow
of a clear night.
Rain, beating
upon the bruised shoulder
of a crippling day.
Hope, bated to a speck
but never dead.

Emissaries of the Unsaid

I stroll into the dim halls of the stuffy Akashic Library, and take a seat, waiting to be assigned purpose and meaning, in the margins of a deceased poet's tome. Do I blend with The Romantics, The Transcendentalists, or The Beats?

Do I await my peers' death, so our words can be pressed into the same musty volume, a gilded title binding us together, our own lexicon and chronology for future poets to unearth?

It is as though we weren't plucking verses from a numinous sky. As if we weren't transcribing lines whispered hastily and naggingly by incorporeal scribes.

Because somewhere today, a woman cries. And also today, a man sinks in the quicksand of his own silence. Because a snowflake doesn't fall sheer and shapeless into a bed of its own, because a helpless child must not die without a whimper from the earth.

An Ocean of Sky

Hushed, the ennui of a winter day.
My hands reach above the water.
Wind brushes my fingertips
with rose gold aquarelles.
Poised, they stand,
for their sacred rite,
to strip the slate of somber light,
replace it with serene blues
of a balmy Sunday afternoon.
Slowly, they dress the clouds
in halcyon white velveteen,
make them giddy with shiny gills,
and let them swim, swim away.

Tame Under the Live Oak

Morning breaks, atoning for the blind night.
Feral horses frolic in the marshy expanse
of a once-Spanish shore. For every shift
in pressure, we know the storm
charges toward us, ominous yet agleam.

Its caution etched in our braided manes,
we dash up-dune to the old live oak. Huddled,
our noses kiss the bark, tails exposed.

We've weathered hundreds of hurricanes
in this pilgrimage of standing firm,
our hooves inured to the stiff, wet sand,
our hardy skin, a keen barometer
of the chilling, surging wind.

Almost Love

Each dawn, we stirred
to the ethereal flute
of the Wood Thrush.
Your angelic face blushed
with content—your limbs,
a weight on my slender frame.

A filling silence,
the murmur of a pure spring
winding along the lush banks
of our almost love.
You don't know
how moon daisies glow
in the fifth dimension
of our anemoia.

We inhale the redolence
of elusive art—
quixotic and over
before it starts.

Intimacy is a Doting Genie

Let's nurture the poetic—
the ogling numen
baking our dough. He dips
into practicalities, as we sleep.
We have never been so close.
Let the balsamic moon
infuse your wounds.
They are old and scarred,
bleached by the caring sun,
warning us to touch lightly,
or leave very well alone.

This soul overlap, six-foot auras
mingling in the kitchen—
your orange zest thinly spread
over my guarded indigo.
Spearlike candor wounds less
than veiled deceit. Here I am,
a transparency of thought
tinted by space and time,
looking your way
across the way—smiling.

Unknotted

I hide in the dark side of a miracle,
beneath its shadow, at half-past dusk.
This rain of shallow reasons undoes me,
watering my tenacious winter flowers.

I offer you a truce in my embrace,
in the purple veins of a nebula
revealed in a saffron flower. Beyond
the insipid dusk of a surrendered breath,

I am. No more do wreaths hang at my door
with their tangled lavender loops
but leaves still thunder on my steel roof,
deepening the night—unlinking me from you.

La Colombe

Like the hands of the sundial,
they come, seamless and punctual,
just and sinners caught
on their ominous wingspan.
An onyx pet stands alert
on Shiva's shoulders.

Oh, Destroyer!
Raise your hand and summon back
your wounded starling
from our MidHeaven.

Nod once from your lotus perch
and behold, war needles faint,
spent, on the crimson sea,
as a child with owl eyes weeps—
a famished release dove
restless in his hands.

Battle's Yield

From your generous hands, they feast,
the feeder-of-ravens and the ring-giver[5].
Minute and adrift on the "M" of your palm,
(militant *"muerte,"* the indelible mark).

You cast them down to Earth, pig-bellied,
to be trodden upon by their kin.
Innocent giants, battle-bred, unaware of death—
their sole breath, Angel White Lilacs,
infusing the ridges of a forsaken matrix.

---

[5] Kennings: ring-giver: king, feeder-of-ravens: warrior

Quiet Quitting of the Housewife

I left long ago, and no one saw me.
A ghost glides my slippers about,
juliennes red peppers, serves stir-fry
over white rice—quiet as ash—
sipping herbal tea at the end of a long

S...............I.............G...........H..........

This slow-burning rapture of vital breath;
unseen arches and braided serpents wreathe.
Today, I rest in the flatline in between.

I immolated long ago, flames unseen, pass by.
Yet something dwells in this vacant, burning bowl.
A flick of fire sometimes erupts through
the silent, lonely spell—its smoky warmth
curling softly toward the open door.

Perhaps someday, someone will notice,
gather my ashes, and scatter them
with gentle hands, over the still swan-road[6].

---

[6] Kenning - swan-road: sea, ocean

overcast evening
moon hisses behind the clouds
I let my cat in

Crushed Under my Soles

Magnolias fell prematurely this year,
ignored in their bloom's fleeting lure.
Sidestepping their crushed hearts,
I blame the gloom—a punch-drunk chill,
still in flight.

Veering on the path to restful beds,
I fault the brave, who forge ahead,
without a nod from the ebullient,
unseeable Goddess, without the comfort
of her doting elf-glory rub[7].

---

[7] Kenning - elf-glory: sun

Rolling the Hours

Missing a spark, a damp, hewn oak
yawns loudly in the quiet family room.
A Netflix character narrates the climb—
not in gold, but in minds ablaze.
I trace their steps, but stay where I am.
Where can I go that I haven't been?
What is left for me to wager
on this checkered dice-ship?[8]

---

[8] Kenning: dice-ship: gameboard

A Pinch of Oregano

My inheritance is a jar
of hand-ground Oregano,
a gift from my late aunt.

Like her, my mother,
and her mother before her,
were attuned to Earth's balms—

knowing how to soothe a fleeting ache
with a twirl of leaves, or banish a headache
with their praying hands.

Yet, when the hungry shadow consumed her
like a dying flame, no "*ensalmo*" could help.[9]
Only a draught-of-giants whirled[10],
exalting her final moments.

Angels waited at her bedside,
unseen to all but her.
Troubled winds paid their respects,
as she closed her eyes.

Her fragrant oregano, an endearing salve,
now perfumes my distant kitchen.
I use it sparingly, to make her essence last.

---

[9] home remedy, or rub, administered with prayer

[10] Kenning - draught-of-giants: sudden poetic realization

Return of the Sea Goddess

In a distant realm,
the unhindered sway
of the broad-hipped brine,
shapely mermaids
keep its mysteries
from the unworthy.
Coral castles congregate,
raising their arms in reverence,
as *Yemayá* glides to the shore[11],
seeking vengeance
astride her sea-steed[12].

---

[11] *Yemayá: Santería* goddess of the ocean

[12] Kenning: sea-steed: ship

Acts of Service as My Love Language

The sun grins at the money tree.

I open the front door,
let warmth in.
I pluck a withered leaf,
and buy you a celestial melody
sung by the Cherubim.

I buy you a dream,
a thrilling reverie
fashioned to your whims—
enduring fantasy
as long as you live.

Next, I secure a sanctuary,
a peaceful haven to call your own.
A resting place at road's end,
where peace is sown.

With the remaining coin, I get a chest,
to keep my treasures,
and the anvil-of-joy, shimmering light[13],
you gave me as a prize.

---

[13] Kenning: anvil-of-joy: heart

Unbowed

Were I to cower, crestfallen
beneath a weeping willow,
to brave the grief-of-the-elm-tree[14],
remind me of the palm.
It neither sways nor breaks
when whipped by the wind.
It claims little space
as it aims for space,
making fruit from salt
in the scalding sand.

If I ever falter,
remind me of who I am.

---

[14] Kenning: grief-of-the-elm-tree: storm

Ice Fossil

I am here because you perceive me.
Before that, I was but a speck...

or a grinning statue in a hibernal garden,
camouflaged by pines, draped in verdigris.

Perhaps I animated my own fairy realm,
expanding tiny stories with my eponym.

Or I emerged from your rib,
and you've been aching since.

Encased in the sea-thatch of your brain[15],
flash-frozen, I will remain.

---

[15] **Kenning: sea-thatch: ice**

daffodils break ground
spring crowns through Mother Earth's womb—
the matrix reloads

Compost

You have withered in me.
Skin to compost, to mush—
under piles of inane words.
I never did see your leaves
sunbathing in the Spring.
I didn't hold your hands
more than once
before the blinding twilight.

All I bury thrives
in the corpse-fjord of my mind[16].
Heaped detritus feeds
this fecund frenzy
of forgotten feelings.
I exhume you with
a caring invocation of breath,
so we may bathe,
release the fetid scent
of decayed love,
and be on our way.

---

[16] Kenning: corpse-fjord: grave

Fatigued by the Ephemeral

Crawling toward maybe—
uncertainty in stride.
The cherry tree weds anew
in pristine white.
Clustered petals revive and deepen
this transient delight.

A Clematis vine rushes
to fasten a soft, sheer blouse,
sashaying into a buoyant
dressing room.

I lend them my lattice shoulder,
and guide them to the heights—
to unfold and wither anew
upon my weary crown.

Fair-weather Hymn

Spring, a slow, halfhearted grin,
the quasi-warmth of an Aries flame.
No forests ablaze.
Trees don their cardigans
and unglue their eyes with disdain.

So do we...

lukewarm embers of a summer fling.
Our pale skin craves the inferno
of the Leo sun, or Cancer's fiery tongue,
wagging molten gold and scarlet scorch.
Parched, we plead for water.

Seasons remain foreign to me, decades
after leaves first revealed their true colors.
I still can't fathom why I live
away from the tropics—here,
where the heavy pendulum swings
from extreme to extreme.

Blocked Throat Chakra

Climbing over a pile of words
that make no sound
for no one utters them
lest there is a shift...

Words, hungry as quicksand
swallowing me up
to the giant knot in my throat.
I look, left and right

but nothing's visible
above my face,
above the ribbons of hair
tying me to the silence.

Wayward Vessels

We are not sure how or why,
our feet grew webbed and cold,
our amphibious skin became
a mood ring circling our thoughts.

The sea erects a barrier
with frigid hands.
beyond which floats
a vast catamaran,

and many ships adrift,
sans captain—
their destinies cast
to the fickle wind.

Spring Cleaning

In the lamplight, we glow amber,
with dry eyes, blinking slowly
to align our skewed silhouettes.
An oversized down blanket shrouds
the smoke of a smoldered flame.

Death is a noun, so we remain,
tethered to our apathy,
diffusing lavender and ylang-ylang
into the putrid silence.

In the daylight, you're absent.
I pull back the blinds, absorbing
the riot of bloom outside my window.
I put on a yellow swing dress,
leave my fleece tights and long-held
doubts at Goodwill's door.

The Catalyst

I knew one day, you'd roam
from proud peak to lowly shore,
mumbling sorrows and regrets
in my deaf ears.

A specter behind my back,
lathering I love yous in my tangled hair—
my fragrant scalp under your fingertips,
tender visions of a quantum leap.

I never thought it would be you
piercing the roof, barefoot above my aura,
wings spread, sword raised high,
urging me to fly.

Fundamental Flaw

Plowing. Digging. Hammering.
Poking holes in the stratosphere
to escape this dimension.
Milking clouds as if they were cows,
tattering the sky's frail night gown.

Loneliness. Asthma gripping our chest,
taking by force what's inherently ours—
a gallon of breath, a bucket of love.
How ironic, our lack of faith,
for we rely on the intangible.

Bribing Destiny

Days rush against the currents
of rivers and winding roads.
We trudge forward, heads bowed,
on parallel paths.

Yours—a clash of pick and shovel,
grating on the growl of a hill.
Mine—a tub of honey and oats,
steeped in vanilla and whispers.

"I'm hungry," you spell in smoke,
a language only I can read. So I leap,
my blistered hands bearing bread,
trying again to lure you home.

After the Rain

And once you learn, I will explain
why we are still parched after the rain.
You still call me to come and play,
to huddle beneath the willow
until it bawls green and long enough.
I have felt your love after the silence,
its ashes quell this arctic drowning.
I am no lighter for this catharsis,
no freer for your goodbye.

Wild and Fruitless

In empty classrooms, irony
rings its rusty handbell,
years removed from learning minds,
I hearken as lines parade,
sequined and overmade.

Why is the Pacific so angry,
the Caribbean Sea so still?
Why would climate protestors
spray-paint Stonehenge? Why,
oh why, rush an adamantine death?
I, too, shall come when it calls,
but not yet.

I'm too busy pulling weeds,
watching dainty flowers grow,
exterminating pineberries
that fruit but once,
stretching their arms tenfold,
multiplying as if dying,
only to spring again
at the faintest hint of warmth.

Proof of Love

He spoke in long sentences,
as if to flood the rotting wood
in this endless hollow.
Drink, I said,
glassfuls of this homebrew.
Tomorrow, we'll still be here,
trimming wheat to grow more grass,
tilling the earth in labor
for one more proof of love.
We were never enough,
so we blame and probe her daily,
tainting her innocence,
like faithful crows.

Empty Tomb

Don't seek me in this house
of thatch and pine,
where I merge with the walls
of ears and eyes.
Don't offer your quilt
of bruised utopias,
its tight fabric affixed
with loose stitching.
Don't weigh me on your scales
of specious justice,
my childlike wrists
restrained by metaphor.
The wristwatch you once gifted
has ceased its ticking.
I keep it in my chest
of rumbling storms.

Beyond the Threshold

Morning light, unsung benefactress,
with mesh hands, you sift through
fine wishes and coarse deceit.
I shy away from this flood of clarity,
unled and upset, ensconced
in my cocoon of ceaseless becoming.
Hold me, so I may breathe, muster
a plunge into the aerial seas,
backstroking away from death
into bygone, quixotic frenzies.

Curves of the Lemniscate

Lost, I wade through
the emerald gleam of memory,
the golden gerund of a kiss.
Tiny fractals of a tapestry
unfold, dazed and thirsty.
Loose sands of captive wind,
a lemniscate's boundless curves.
Time, encapsulated primrose
of midnight eureka. Fear,
locked and loaded in the pistol
of a seamless breath.
Boneless arms and spine sway,
like shiny ribbons bent to infinity.

an Eastern Bluebird
feasts on a wild berry branch—
grasshoppers exhale

Severed Radicle

Stacked rocks and concave mirrors—
I can't tell my face from a river's swell.
Come tomorrow, my roots might hang
upside down, hairs flailing in the pristine air,
waving at a timber lorry.

I've forgotten how to grow in the dark.
This broken radicle crawls
beyond my professed blindness,
through the helpless, trembling soil,
and the patient, cold groundwater
creeping below.

Lament of Endless Starts

Timely   rebirth,   unfolding
of a leaf, resurging   patterns,
vein-deep, resurrect   the apex.

Don't wake me from my rooted sleep.
I don't have it in me   to chase
the sky for a sip   of   sun,

one more odyssey, one more   storm
bearing down on my tired   bones.
Call me   when everyone is   gone.

The Hand We Were Dealt

Whisky and cigars in a dimly lit room...
Must the carpet be crimson velvet,
wood paneling smothering sweaty walls?

I half-inhale this ancient world
of patriarchy and lingering smoke.
How long must I hold my nose?

A bodybuilder toad deals the cards.
I get them all, so I can steer
where the King falls, where Aces land.

I shuffle—more times than intuition calls,
surveying each poker face, seeking clues
in the curling wisps hovering above us.

They, too, have all the cards. We all shuffle,
with almighty hands, but ours isn't a game
of mere luck and fateful chance.

The dealer exhales once more,
eyeing us from left to right. He hops away,
paws empty, leaving us to our trance.

a besotted star
piercing darkness with its sword—
a celebration

Seeds of Revelation

Analects vanish from the library
of fantasy, one about a girl
lost in a sunflower maze.
The deeper she ventures,
the closer to Genesis—
a zero-point seat where she perceives:

how a seed becomes sustenance,
promise, and might,
how a marvelous bird
melds with uncertainty,
and a titan succumbs
to the fat tails of time.

Her frail fingers outlast
the final meteor bursting
upon her summer dress
before journey's end.

Clockwork of Memory

Heel fissures graze the shards,
yet not a drop of blood spills.
Your voice cracks faintly
at the other end of the line.

Movement—your shoes tap,
waiting beyond the threshold.
Silence, denser than a black hole,
starving for sensation.

Love, stubborn and irretrievable,
unyielding and insatiable—
consuming all in its path,
as greedy as the black hole.

The View from the Islet

Pearlescent tail
slivering through the gloom.
An amorphous moon
pulled by a seahorse...

Eyes intent
on anything but here—
sparkling swords
of spent tomorrows...

We slip on a dragon.
Its golden blossom prints
scatter on the water,
refracting our needs.

They emblazon fractals
on our loose kimonos[17],
with dawn's rising ochres—
a sigil of our becoming.

---

[17] Inspired by a painting by Japanese artist Hikari

carefree, mortal men
pandoras in the meadow
serendipity

Dead-air Magenta

Follow a line into the knotted night.
How I mourned you in the rain,
music notes swallowed by concrete.
You heard me and closed your eyes,
slept through the white noise.
Pink moons wouldn't soften
the jagged horizon in my palm.
I watched you sleep in the reflection
of the lake upon my hand.
The cherry tree won't fade
its still-air, hardy inferno—
irony taints the ivory landscape.
Connect the dots to the very end of us,
to the gates of this poetic hyperspace.

Summer Slopes

Canoodling in a gondola—sky lift.
The snow retreats, cowering
from the summer heat.
Shoes off, we levitate downhill,
inexorably drawn to a bed of wet grass.
Alone at last, on lovelorn meadows.
Shrubs grow jealous; they'll never roll
on our corridor of truce and quarrels.

Aftershock of Reverence

At the very least, we have the cottage,[18]
a stone of reverence on solid ground.
Days march swiftly beyond my grasp of wisdom,
crushing the purple dome aster beaming beneath.

It was always us. That much, we know.
Light breaks slowly over the covered bridge.
I may nest in this makeshift haven,
birdsong waning, crooning a baby spring.

But home lingers, unlived, amid an aftershock
of whispers, like the failed logic of a lullaby.
Sleep, my love, this undeclared madness.
The night yet whimpers, waiting in line.

---

[18] reference to "The Cottage," published in Antonia Wang's debut poetry collection "Love Bites."

Making a Mark

It all makes sense
spelled out in ink.
We wield the wet strokes
of this fresh calligraphy,
yet not the words.

Hold a random pen,
to inscribe the delicate.
Chisels and mallets
for the unwilling stone.

Symbols must emerge, regardless.
Else why do we linger,
primed and prepped
in this blank canvas?

To voice our grievances
at the feral morning,
devoid of meaning
till the tame, brown dusk.

Immortals' Play

We walk backward from death,
bringing tokens from Heaven or Hades:
dream flotillas piled high in a wheelbarrow,
the candlelight of an orphan flower
growing legs in a kitchen vase—
a lover's name learned in hindsight.

Flesh-bound Chronos, minute yet mighty,
ticks and tallies what eludes the eyes.
So we forget the working of the tides,
our mother's favorite meal on Sunday night.
We forget it all, but time keeps track.

We were ancient before childhood's dawn.
We were happy before we learned words.

If It Fits the Bill

Come live with me
where black swans reign—
aristocrats waltzing
on ponds of apathy,

where the lotus is more
an emblem than a flower,
and bills upon the water
fail to stir a ripple...

where muddied echoes ribbon
the stillness of our necks,
and time unspools its colors
in our silent reflection.

I Told You, But Did I Show You?

Weigh my heart against a feather.
Did I let you love me?
Tip-toes in the creek,
hair free in a tangled bounce.
Hands. Zooming down the highway,
ten lives a minute.
Acanthus tongues, dissolving
like powdered sugar in your smile.
Did you let me love you
as you swore you would?
Nails etching a golden ring in the
open chest of our young mid-heaven,
birds of different feathers, gliding.

Choosing the Season

We won't know until we bloom
archipelagos in the irises,
glinting a brand new hue...
I see you more today,
since limbo is a place I can draw.
I need no ladder to ascend.
I have tamed this turquoise wave
of silken loss. Though it is Fall
somewhere, and all that ever leaves
has met its doom, I choose to bloom.

Older But Not Wiser

Recollection feels unearthly.
I had forgotten how your breath
steams the glass window,
blurring my view of the garden.
Oak and pine merge in the warm distortion—
a sudden dawning. I call out to the far forest
from this point of mercy,
pleading for one more summer of love,
before the fog clears.

Yet color drains from the ice
into the puzzled field. There is no path
of liberation from this ancient labyrinth.
Whether or not you hold my hand,
we're still lost among the same trees.
They know our names, our scent,
the squelch of our footfalls upon their sobs.
They, too, are lonely... and lost.

water flows upstream
salmon don't know where to swim—
contrarians' cure

Solar Maximum

Clear day,
a warm corona swaddles my bones.

Freedom
within towering megaliths...

Death—
mere chatter between lives,
apropos of nothing... we

Dance.
From plié to arabesque,
a humble flexion, an exaltation...

Touch.
I am melting stone in your candor,
at risk of iridescence, as the Aurora swirls.

Identity Crisis

In a vacant alley between two thoughts,
the Logos blinks—infinite, infinitesimal.
A sapling breaks through the pavement
with a whisper. What will I be today,
a flower or a weed? It isn't up to me.
I wait for a sign. Footsteps and voices
approach, then fade. A gentle hand strokes
my stem. A flower, I must be a flower!
Joyful, I sway. My roots release their hold.
I can run freely! But wait, I lack feet.
I falter and faint. Withering, I concede
I wasn't a flower after all, but indeed a weed.

Fluid Constructs

Sudden birth mid-flight...
Timelines crumble like Lego towers,
their structure, a fleeting mirage.
No shape is forced
through the eye of a needle.

Land is promised to no one,
yet we plead for an acre of rain.
I've dissolved into this notion
more than once.

Someone else will reap my harvest,
ripe and ready when I'm gone.
Emergency landing—
no one noticed I was born.

Wrapped in Cellophane

Crescent moon,
lunula of the ailing sky,
cradle and lullaby
of the cherubim.
With their melodies,
our hope sleeps
snuggled in pathos that drape
lightly over this ache.

We do not break, my love,
we bathe in celestial shrapnel
and emerge pristine and fragrant
among jasmine beds—
wiser in our faith,
softer in our pain.

Terrarium Prisoner

Her face in the glass,
a faint breath's trace.

Her tears contour the day,
falling in parallel.

Cobwebs imprison tulips
in the terrarium of her eyes.

Don't tell her she is alive
only in a stranger's dream.

Don't suggest she is confined,
condensed under lamplight.

Zip Code Comparisons

Pondering a new life,
a new skyline to behold from afar—
acreage to grow in all directions,
away from sirens and headlights,
the constant chatter and critique
on either shoulder.
A place where the land
hasn't felt my step,
and the river hasn't learned
the flow of my unwavering curves.

Sunset Pairings

Drop by drop, I fill this ocean.
Looming mountains reflected
in the sharp crystal of its shore.
More and more, I collect
everything I can gather
with outstretched arms,
until twilight sags and dips
the sun in melted chocolate.
I take the sweet and sour bite,
wash it down with pinot noir,
think of all the great pairings
that will never see the light.
The magpie's wingspan stretches
under a sequined cluster of sighs—
unmeasurable, unmistakable.

severed cords dangle
from flaccid solar plexus—
a soft remembrance

Cycle of Be-Longing

To hear your laugh over the yodel
of a Quaking Aspen—its trembling wave
of hearts fanning the searing sky.
We cling to silver threads of dreams,
pluck fruit too soon from the Tree of Life—
before another takes a bite,
before we remember our hunger.

Our thirst, we carry (in heavy buckets),
rambling through the monochrome desert.
An oasis shimmers with scripted soulmates:
one with the picket fence,
one with forbidden fruit,
and one holding the mirror
to our warped reflection.

We walk on by—not today.
Today is for wandering thirsty and alone,
our clay bucket heavier with each complaint.
A glance at the sky—maybe it will rain,
and it does. We cry for days, for eons,
until we're empty, our buckets brimming,
our fruit scattered from the aging tree—
its mature seed, tomorrow's creation.

Millennia with a Mercurial Babysitter

Permission to be me,
petal of the flower moon,
flash and feature of a periodic bloom.
Elsewhere, stygian chandeliers shroud
the indiscernible ground.
Not here. This transient spotlight
reminds neglectful Gods
we, children, are still outside,
playing late in the elements,
ragged and muddied,
with no one to call us home.

Thriving Quietly, Without Rain

A bath bomb of blue...
I bathe in streaked, still waters.
Rain incites the green. I grin.
It is May. Thunder growls far away.
Hungry ghosts loiter around my door.
They're too shy to knock
but know they will be fed,
for lichen thrives on air.
This affair with the wind,
unsung keystone of faith.
I bathe—lathering blue,
rinsing clear my freckled pelt.

Warm Waters on My Cheeks

Hold me gently,
arrest of tenderness,
epiphany of an exhale.

Bliss-spun menagerie,
velvet hangs
beyond a wistful morrow.

You lay me softly
on fecund clouds,
and they rain.

Upside down—I float,
my face to your sun,
my crescent to your night.

Return to Sender

To shrink a smile to pursed lips,
so its sharp blade no longer cuts.
These rays are too bright for eyes
that spent years in a cave.
The built-in lasso unspools slowly
from my open chest. It pulls me out
to anoint new ground in a hopeful ramble.
It's time to move again
away from myself, closer to me.

weeping willow's tears
more habit than mere sadness
maples' crimson blush

Dawning of a New Melody

It runs on—unstrung
enjambment of uncured days.
This pang, a diurnal brooch,
worn in place of a heart,
pinned on stoic corners—
unseen by the naked eye
or a *clair de lune* logic
that never reached beyond
its frigid fingertips.

A gown of graduated light
slips over the charcoal mist,
as if asking for a dance
before the music plays.
Smooth, dainty feet
tiptoe the broken railings,
in a haste to jump—leap
toward the strumming
of a restored Spanish guitar.

The Sound of Surrender

We are residues of a pulse,
invisible to ourselves.
We made our peace with this
before we were born.

Failing to remember
doesn't slow damnation.
Lofty speech is not knowledge.
Stark silence is not wisdom.

Even Spring has a Fall.
Ask magnolias how to let go
without making noise—
without an iota of regret.

Defaced

Whatever we had was lost
in the throes of late-season lingo.
Scalded by excess—
for one can love too much.
I held the pendulum
when it swung my way
and wouldn't let go.
The world tilted and spilled,
blistering, over my face.
I am defaced without you,
forever seeking my reflection
in puddles of tenuous light
and silted grace.

Final Cut

Once it's over, you will know,
it was love, harvested
like a calla lily,
with a sharp moon blade,
displayed in a dimly lit room,
in a weighted, tall glass vase—
enduring, as an orchid,
the yellowing of neglect...
the romantic, wordless end.

Final Tribute

We grew wary... occult
like the Timberwolf moon
on misty mornings,
our exuberance relenting
with each unspoken word.

Our purpose was clear
a hundred howls ago:
to camouflage our hope
with the summer greenery,
to never raise a plume
to the illegible sky,
to conform to silence.

Yet mumblings turned
to shouts pounding within,
for a heart can be a prison,
and reasons can be bars.
Mondays turned into Fridays,
into next month,
into despondency.

The echoes of your voice
have long since died.
I place a single rose
on your smooth marble tomb—
no tears, no goodbye.

Tidal Reverence

And now you are gone,
after many salt baths,
my kneeling in water,
clamoring to *Yemayá*[19].
The unwritten verse now complete,
I lay my plume.

A white, inkless feather
rests on my right ear,
balanced by the scales of the wind.
Justice was not the aim
of this penitential limerence.
Neither was love.

It was the water itself,
its gracious curves embracing mine,
a stripping of blue in the blue.
A chance to nod my head
at the old, sharp horizon—
its line always deeper than the sea.

Watching the stark, bald eagles
soar overhead, loud
in their convocation.
"Fly with us," they say, and I follow—
for I am lighter and freer now
than the plume on my ear.

---

[19] *Yemayá: Santería* goddess of the ocean

Acknowledgments

Versions of these pieces first appeared in the following journals:

"Forging Light" — *Fevers of the Mind*
"Eden" — *Fevers of the Mind*
"Forward" — *Literary Revelations Journal*
"A Silent Banquet" — *Fevers of the Mind*
"For Lily" — *The New Stylus*
"Gangrene" — *SpillWords Press*
"Sepia Stains" — SpillWords Press
"Portrait of a Missing Kiss" — *Literary Revelations Journal*
"Two Dolls and Three Kings" — *The Bluebird Word*
"Quiet Quitting of the Housewife" — *The New Stylus*
"Dead-air Magenta — *The New Stylus*

The following haiku were published in *Petals of Haiku: An Anthology by Literary Revelations:*

"I Shush My Loud Heart"
"Golden Beach Sojourn"
"From Derriere to Amber Coast"
"Past the Naked Tree"

The following haiku were published in *Jewels of Serendipity: An International Anthology of Formal English-Language Haiku by Hyphen Journal:*

"I Let Love Happen"
"Moon Hisses Behind the Clouds"
"The Matrix Reloads"
"Grasshoppers Exhale"
"Contrarian's Cure"

My heartfelt thanks to Vanessa Anderson for editing this poetry collection with a sharp eye for language and a talent for streamlined expression.

I am deeply grateful to the #vss365 Writing Community on X, to the journals and editors who have published my work, and to my readers for their support.

About the Author

Antonia Wang, a bilingual poet and yogi from the Dominican Republic, now calls the United States home. Her writing explores the interplay of nature and emotion, celebrates hidden nuances, and embraces self-reflection.

Her poetry has appeared in numerous journals, publications, and even a high school textbook. Antonia's expanding collections in English and Spanish include *Love Bites*, *In the Posh Cocoon*, *Retrospectiva 2020*, *Things I Could Have Said in One Line But Didn't*, *Palette*, *Matices*, and *Taste of Salt*.

Visit Antonia at biteslove.com or follow her on X @tuttysan.

www.ingramcontent.com/pod-product-compliance
Lightning Source LLC
LaVergne TN
LVHW051553080426
835510LV00020B/2965